j551.3   Bramwell, Martyn
BRA   Glaciers and
c.1   Ice Caps

EARTH SCIENCE LIBRARY

GLACIERS AND ICE CAPS

MARTYN BRAMWELL

Franklin Watts

London · New York · Toronto · Sydney

© 1986 Franklin Watts

First published in Great Britain by
Franklin Watts
12a Golden Square
London W1

First published in the USA by
Franklin Watts Inc.
387 Park Avenue South
New York, N.Y. 10016

First published in Australia by
Franklin Watts Australia
14 Mars Road
Lane Cove
NSW 2066

UK ISBN: 0 86313 410 6
US ISBN: 0-531-10178-9
Library of Congress Catalog Card
No: 85-52046

Printed in Belgium

Designed by Ben White

Picture research by Mick
Alexander

Illustrations:
Chris Forsey
Colin Newman/Linden Artists

Photographs:
Ardea 16*t*, 28
Bruce Coleman 16*b*
GeoScience Features 10
Robert Harding 9*b*, 25*r*
Frank Lane 5, 9*t*, 11*b*, 17, 19*r*, 24, 29
Natural Science Photos 18
John Noble 1, 4
Seaphot back cover, 23, 26
Charles Swithinbank 11*t*, 19*l*, 25*l*
Woodmansterne 15*b*, 21
ZEFA 8, 12, 14, 15*t*

EARTH SCIENCE LIBRARY

GLACIERS AND ICE CAPS

MARTYN BRAMWELL

Contents

Lands of ice and snow

The polar regions are vast wilderness areas of bare rock and biting winds, of snowstorms, **ice caps** and **glaciers**. Antarctica is a continent twice the size of Australia and covered by the world's largest **ice sheet**. The Arctic is a complete contrast. Most of it is ocean, almost completely encircled by land and covered for most of the year by thick floating ice. Here, too, ice sheets cover much of the surrounding land, and in both regions slow-moving rivers of ice called glaciers pour down the mountains and into the sea.

South of the ice zone lies a barren treeless region called the **tundra**. The ground is frozen to depths of hundreds of feet in places, but in summer the thin surface layer melts enough to allow mosses and lichens to grow.

▽ Alpine climbers look out over a cloud-capped world of ice and rock from the summit of Monte Rosa on the border between Italy and Switzerland.

The tops of high mountains are like miniature polar regions. Their upper slopes are clothed in mosses, lichens and grasses, just like the Arctic tundra, while higher still there is only windswept rock, snow and ice. The mountains have been shaped by their glaciers, and even in parts of the world no longer covered in ice, mountain regions still bear the marks of the glaciers and ice caps that covered them in the distant past.

▷ Icicles formed by the trickling **meltwaters** of summer hang from a wind-polished ice wall in Antarctica.

A mountain glacier

▽ As the newly formed ice starts to move from its bowl-shaped cirque, deep crevasses called **bergschrunds** open up along the back wall.

Moisture that drops from clouds over mountains usually falls as snow, and in the permanent cold of the mountain world very little melts. Instead it collects in hollows and becomes packed hard into a dense white mass called **névé**, or firn. Very slowly the névé changes into hard, clear ice.

But ice is not quite as solid as it seems. Slowly, under its own weight, it starts to flow downhill.

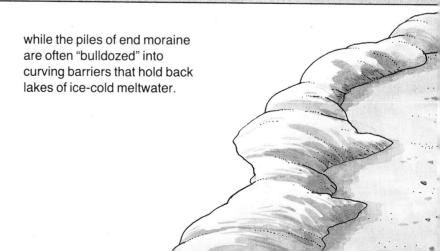

▷ The huge load of rock debris frozen into the glacier gives the moving ice tremendous power to erode, or wear away, the underlying rocks. But beyond the end, or **snout**, of the glacier this moraine debris is dumped. The edge moraines are left as ridges along the valley sides, while the piles of end moraine are often "bulldozed" into curving barriers that hold back lakes of ice-cold meltwater.

▽ The glacier sides are littered with piles of sharp rock fragments that tumble from the peaks and ridges above. Each time two glaciers merge together, another dark stripe of rock debris, or moraine, is added to the once-white surface of the ice. The number of stripes in a large glacier gives a good idea of the number of smaller glaciers that have joined together.

As it slips from its collecting hollow, it scrapes away at the rock, gradually widening and deepening the hollow into a bowl-shaped **cirque**.

On gentle slopes glacier ice flows quite smoothly. But where the slope suddenly steepens, the ice cannot take the strain. It breaks, and deep cracks called **crevasses** open up. On very steep slopes the whole ice-flow may break up into an **icefall**, with ice blocks the size of houses separated by gaping crevasses.

As it moves downhill, the glacier picks up tons of broken rock. Some is frozen into the bottom of the ice. Some falls from the rock faces above and is carried along at the sides of the ice-flow. This rock debris gives the glacier its power to **erode**, or wear away, the sides and bottom of its valley. Later the rock debris is dumped in the lowlands in a series of landscape features called **moraines**.

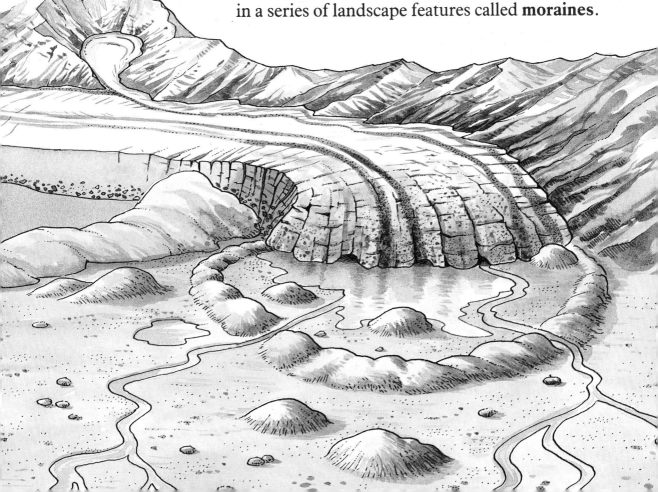

How glaciers move

If you hit a large block of ice with a hammer, it feels rock hard. Showers of ice fragments fly off in all directions. Yet when ice builds up to a thickness of about 25 m (82 ft), it behaves very differently. It starts to move downhill under its own weight – bending and flowing around obstacles in its path, rather like toothpaste squeezed from a tube.

Scientists call this movement "plastic flow," and ice can move in this way as long as it travels slowly. But when a glacier pours down a steep slope, or has to flow around a sharp bend in its valley, it breaks – just as modeling clay will break if you stretch it too quickly. This is why glaciers often break up into crevasses and ice-falls when they spill over the edge of a cirque and down a steep mountain face.

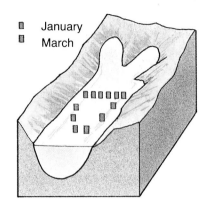

January
March

△ Markers placed on the glacier show how fast the ice is moving. The greatest speed is always in mid-stream.

▽ A group of small cirques feed their ice into a spectacular icefall high in the Swiss Alps.

◁ Dark bands of moraine show where many smaller glaciers have joined the main ice-stream of the Kennicott Glacier in the Wrangell Mountains of southern Alaska.

In the very cold polar regions glacier ice is always well below freezing point. Most of the glaciers are frozen fast to the rocks below. They cannot slide, so nearly all their movement is by plastic flow. But in the warmer **temperate** regions, like North and South America, Europe and New Zealand, mountain glaciers have another way of moving. They have a built-in lubricating system which helps the ice slide over the rocks below. Their ice is not as cold as the polar ice. It does not stick fast to the rocks. And there is nearly always some water present underneath the glacier. Some of this comes from melt-water trickling down through cracks in the ice, especially during the warm summer months. But ice melts under pressure, and much of the water is produced by melting beneath the glacier, where the ice is pressed hard against the valley floor.

Because of this layer of water, most temperate glaciers move much faster than polar glaciers. Their speeds vary from a few inches a day to as much as 30 m (100 ft) a day on steep slopes. And because they actually slide and scrape over the ground, they are able to change the shape of the land very dramatically.

▽ Crevasses are a constant danger to mountaineers and polar travelers. Here, in Antarctica, a member of a survey team marks a safe route over a crevasse bridged by hard, wind-blown snow.

Melt streams and ice caves

In winter a glacier is quiet for most of the time. The silence is broken only occasionally by the loud crack of ice breaking under the stress of movement, or by the rattling of pieces of rock tumbling from the ridges above. Constant cold winds and frequent snowfalls keep the upper layers of the glacier very cold. The temperature may be well below freezing point down to a depth of 10 m (33 ft) or more. The glacier surface is dry. The only liquid water is the thin layer beneath the glacier, formed by ice melting under the enormous pressure of the glacier's weight.

In summer the glacier seems much more alive. The sound of running water provides a constant background, and the signs of rushing water are everywhere. Warm winds and sunshine melt the surface snows of surrounding peaks and soften the upper layers of ice on the glacier itself. The glacier

△ Milky-white streams of meltwater gush from cave entrances in the snout of a glacier in the Italian Alps. The glacier here is shrinking, slowly retreating back up its valley as the ice melts and dumps its load of angular frost-shattered rock.

is covered in running streams of meltwater, wearing channels in the ice and cascading down crevasses and potholes into the depths of the glacier.

Much of this water finds its way right down to the bottom of the glacier, where it increases the amount of lubrication. This is why mountain glaciers move much more quickly in summer than they do in winter.

In the higher parts of the glacier these melt streams are crystal clear. But as they flow through the glacier, they pick up soil and particles of rock, as well as the very fine **rock flour** produced by the constant grinding of the ice and rocks. When the streams finally emerge from the snout of the glacier, they may be any color from milky white to dark brown, depending on the amount of mud and silt they have picked up on their journey.

△ The sculpturing effect of rushing water can produce incredibly beautiful channels and caves inside a glacier.

◁ The whole story of a meltwater stream is told in this photograph. Pouring from the glacier snout, the melt stream has cut a deep notch in the hillside before winding its way across the flat coastal plain. Where it flows into the sea, the very fine rock flour is swept along the coast, clearly separating the glacier waters from the blue seawater.

11

Landscapes carved by ice

One of the main features of a landscape carved by glaciers is the contrast between the smooth rounded shapes of the valley floors and the hard outlines of the peaks and ridges above.

The reason for this lies in the way the two landscapes are shaped. The lowlands are formed mainly by scraping, while the peaks are created by the shattering effect of freezing water.

When water freezes, it expands; that is, it takes up more space than it does in liquid form. During the day, when snow melts in the sun, trickles of water run into the tiny cracks in the rocks. Then, when the water freezes at night, it expands, pushing against the sides of the cracks with enormous force and gradually widening them.

△ The classic "pyramid" shape of the Matterhorn in the Swiss Alps was formed by several cirques meeting back-to-back.

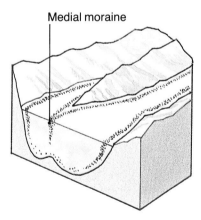

Medial moraine

△ When two glaciers flow together, two of their **lateral moraines** (the edge moraines) also merge together to form a dark stripe down the middle of the glacier. The new stripe is known as a **medial moraine**. Beneath the ice the ridge separating the two glaciers is smoothed into a long tail that finally disappears.

12

Next day the ice melts and the water runs farther into the cracks, where it freezes again. The process is repeated over and over again until eventually pieces of rock are split off.

Where frost shattering and the grinding action of glaciers attack opposite sides of a mountain ridge, the result is a sharp ridge called an **arête**. The right-hand side of the picture on page 8 is a perfect example. Arêtes also form where two cirques meet side by side. And if a mountain is completely ringed by cirques, their back walls eventually meet and produce a classic pyramid-shaped peak like the Matterhorn.

▽ Long after the glaciers have gone, frost shattering is still the main force of erosion in the highlands. The loose rock debris is building up conical mounds of **scree** along the valley sides. The smooth floor of the valley is now occupied by lakes. The one on the left is at a lower level than that on the right, showing where the glacier cut downward after crossing a band of hard rock.

Scree cone

Glaciated valleys

When a glacier leaves its cirque, it consists of almost pure ice. But as soon as its starts its downward journey, it begins to pick up pieces of rock, from tiny dust-sized particles to huge boulders. Much of the rock falls on to the glacier from the cliffs and rock faces above, but the ice itself also creates broken rock by a process called "plucking." Where the ice moves over a rough rock surface, it tends to stick to it. Then, as the ice moves on, it pulls out any loose bits of rock and carries them away.

▽ A waterfall plunges over the lip of a hanging valley in Switzerland. Tributary glaciers from the cirques in the far distance would have merged and then flowed out of the hanging valley into the main glacial valley filling the foreground.

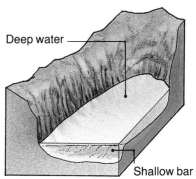

◁ Geiranger Fjord in central Norway. The steep rock walls and deep waters – more than 1,200 m (4,000 ft) in many fjords – are typical. Two hanging valleys can be seen on the right-hand side.

Very soon the sides and bottom of the glacier are studded with frozen-in rock fragments and the glacier has become a powerful excavating tool. As it creeps along, it acts like a gigantic rasp, gouging out millions of tons of earth and rock and leaving behind a deep, wide, U-shaped valley.

Mountain glaciers are often fed by smaller side glaciers or tributaries, just as rivers are. Usually the main glacier has already cut a deep valley for itself and so the smaller tributaries flow into the upper layers of the main glacier. When the ice eventually retreats, these tributary valleys are stranded high up. Instead of joining the main valley at the level of the valley floor, their openings are high up on the valley sides – and so they are called **hanging valleys**.

Where glaciers once plunged down steep valleys into the sea, many gouged their valleys right down to sea level and sometimes even below it. Later, when the ice melted and sea level rose, these valleys were flooded, forming **fjords**. The shelf or bar across the mouth of a fjord marks the end moraine of the original glacier.

△ Lake Windermere in the English Lake District is typical of the long narrow **ribbon lakes** that occupy old glacial valleys. The lake is 16 km (10 miles) long and its southern end is blocked by a glacial end moraine.

15

After the ice

The ice sheets and glaciers of the great Ice Age drew back from Europe and North America more than 10,000 years ago, yet their marks are etched on the landscape for all to see.

In many areas deep scratch marks on exposed surfaces show where the ice scraped over the ground with its captive load of broken rock. In other places huge lumps of rock are found hundreds of miles from their places of origin, carried there on the moving sheets of ice and dumped as the ice melted. They are called glacial **erratics** and they are very useful to scientists tracing the patterns of ice movement in the distant past. Some are simply large boulders, like those of Scottish granite found on a hillside in South Wales. But one famous erratic in Alberta, Canada, is estimated to weigh over 18,000 tons.

△ Although damaged by later erosion, this rock surface shows the high polish caused by the rock flour held in the glacier ice. The deeper scratches were made by larger rock fragments.

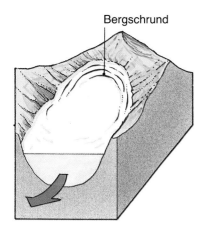

Bergschrund

▷ Almost but not quite! Given a few more thousand years, the glaciers that carved these cirques in the Glacier National Park on the US/Canadian border might have turned this mountain into a classic pyramid like the Matterhorn.

Several granite erratics in the Rhine valley of southern Germany are large enough to have been quarried for building stone!

In mountain regions all over the world there are cirques and valleys long since abandoned by the ice that formed them. The surrounding lowlands are littered with the remnants of glacial moraines and the long wavy bands of sand and gravel, called **eskers**, that were dumped on the ground by rivers flowing beneath the ice.

As well as the ridges and mounds of old glacial moraines, huge areas of land are covered with thick layers of **boulder clay**, or till. These jumbled mixtures of clay, sand, gravel and rocks were once the ground moraines of large ice sheets. In places the boulder clay has been molded and shaped by the still-moving ice into scattered groups of oval whale-backed mounds called **drumlins**.

The normal processes of erosion have altered and softened many of these features, but still they remain – covered with grasslands, forests or fields. They are full of information about an ice-bound world of 10,000 years ago.

△ A huge expanse of "pot-hole" moraine spreads out at the end of the Eldridge Glacier in Alaska. The moraine is a chaotic mass of rock debris and lumps of ice which melt and leave crater-like holes.

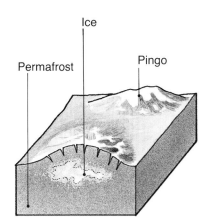

△ The **pingo** is a feature of tundra landscapes, where the soil beneath the thin surface layer is always frozen. Water seeping up from deep in the ground freezes in this **permafrost** layer and heaves the surface into a high dome.

Ice caps and ice sheets

About 97 percent of the water on the face of the earth is seawater. Barely three percent is fresh water, and three-quarters of that is ice and snow. Most of it is locked up in the huge ice sheets of Antarctica and Greenland.

When ice builds up over a mountain region, it fills the valleys. The ice forms a huge dome, pierced only by the jagged peaks of the highest mountains. Up to 50,000 sq km (19,300 sq miles) the dome is called an ice cap. Larger areas of permanent ice are called ice sheets. The largest one in the northern hemisphere is that of Greenland. It is more than 3,350 m (11,000 ft) thick in places.

▽ Several glaciers merge as they pour down into the sea from the high **plateau** ice sheet of the Antarctic **Peninsula**.

△ Hundreds of lakes dot the moraine-covered landscape left by ancient ice sheets in Alaska.

△ **Nunataks**, like these in Antarctica, are the jagged tips of mountains submerged in the ice.

Nearly 85 percent of the world's permanent ice is contained in the great ice sheet of Antarctica – a vast frozen continent larger than Europe and the United States combined. The average thickness of the Antarctic ice is 2,000 m (6,500 ft), and the greatest measured thickness is more than 4,770 m (15,650 ft).

Antarctica's ice accumulates very slowly. Although we think of it as a land of howling snow-storms, this intensely cold continent has less snow than most temperate countries. Most of the blizzards consist of old snow picked up and blown about by the incessant gales. The ice also moves extremely slowly, and many parts of the ice sheet are millions of years old.

Where the ice reaches the coast, squeezed out under its own enormous weight, it pours through the coastal mountain ranges in huge glaciers. In other places, such as the Ross Sea and Weddell Sea, it forms floating **ice shelves**. Their sheer ice cliffs tower 50 m (165 ft) above the water, with their bases hidden 250 m (820 ft) beneath the waves. Sometimes huge blocks of ice break off to form **icebergs**.

19

The Ice Age

▷ If the **Ice Age** returned, so much water would be locked up in the ice sheets that sea level would fall, leaving most of America's ports stranded far from the new coastline.

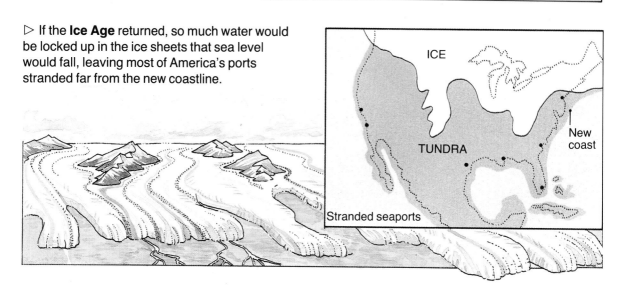

Fifteen thousand years ago the world's average temperatures were a good deal lower than today. Much of North America and northern Europe was covered by thick ice sheets, over a mile thick in places. Even as recently as 10,000 years ago the land now occupied by the cities of Chicago and Montreal, Amsterdam and Copenhagen was buried beneath hundreds of meters of ice. And stretching far to the south of these city sites lay a bleak wilderness of Arctic tundra.

For almost a million years the ice dominated the land. Four times it advanced across the land and then retreated again. Between each Ice Age there was a warmer spell called an interglacial period. When the great ice sheets pulled back about 10,000 years ago, they ended the most recent phase of the Ice Age. And it is important that we do say "most recent" rather than "last," because the warm conditions in Europe and North America today are probably just another interglacial period. We cannot say for sure that the Ice Age is over. It may well return.

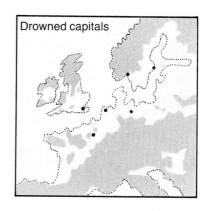

△ If three-quarters of the polar ice melted, floodwaters would reach Chicago from the Gulf of Mexico, and most of the European capitals would be drowned.

20

If the ice did advance again, it could very easily cover the whole of Canada, the northern part of the United States, Britain, Scandinavia and northern Asia. It would also bring tundra conditions back to the great farmland areas of America, Europe and Asia.

Imagine what might happen if the earth's climate swung in the opposite direction and became several degrees warmer. Even a small-scale melting of the polar ice caps would very quickly cause flooding in the Netherlands and northern Germany, in parts of the Middle East, the southern United States and parts of lowland China.

If three-quarters of the polar ice were to melt, the result would be catastrophic. The world's coastlines would be completely redrawn. Most of the world's ports and major cities would be drowned, and a large part of the world's productive farmland would be covered by the sea.

▽ The alternate freezing and melting of large amounts of water during the Ice Ages caused sea level to change by as much as 100 m (320 ft) in some places. If sea level rises, river valleys may be flooded by the sea (below left). If sea level falls, then former coastal features may be left high and dry, like the raised beaches at Gruinard Bay in Scotland (below).

The Arctic region

The north polar region is an ocean, nearly 5,300 km (3,300 miles) across and almost completely surrounded by land. In winter the entire ocean is locked in ice, piled into jagged heaps by the fierce gales and driven in a slow clockwise circulation by the winds and currents. But in summer the ice melts and breaks up. Wide areas of open water appear along the coasts. The warm rays of the sun allow **marine** life to flourish, and for a few brief months the Arctic waters become a rich feeding ground for whales, seals, walruses and seabirds.

The tundra landscape is also transformed. As the ground softens, streams and pools cover the surface. Plant life blossoms into a carpet of mosses, lichens, grasses and flowering plants, alive with the buzzing clouds of insects.

Wildfowl and wading shorebirds arrive in their millions to breed on the tundra. Herds of reindeer, caribou and musk ox wander the plains.

☐ Permanent ice
☐ Seasonal ice

△ The central region of the Arctic Ocean is permanently frozen, but around that zone lies a broad band of seasonal ice – solid in winter but broken into **pack ice** in summer.

▷ Animals that spend most of the year in the Arctic regions are specially adapted to cope with the harsh climate. The musk ox, arctic fox and caribou have dense fur coats. Birds like the ptarmigan have thickly feathered legs and feet. Several animals, like the fox, ptarmigan, hare and ermine, change their coats to white in winter to camouflage them against the snow.

They share the plant food with lemmings, voles and arctic hares. And where there are grazers there are always hunters. Arctic foxes, wolves and ermines stalk the ground, while owls, falcons and gulls patrol overhead.

In winter it is a different story. A few animals – polar bears, musk ox, hares and snowy owls – remain. But for most animals survival means escaping from the cold. Lemmings and shrews survive in burrows beneath the snow. Some of the larger animals **hibernate**, or sleep, through the winter. But most **migrate** to warmer regions. Caribou and reindeer retreat into the forests, while the wildfowl fly south to spend the winter in the temperate zones of Europe, Asia and North America.

△ Icebergs "calved" from the Greenland glaciers are a beautiful sight in good weather – but a hazard to shipping in winter fog and mist.

Life in the Arctic

Beyond the shore the sea bed slopes down gently at first. Then it suddenly plunges steeply to the deep sea bed. The edge of the shallow zone marks the true edge of the continent, and the shallow area is called the **continental shelf**.

Off the North American coast the shelf is 80–250 km (50–150 miles) wide. But off the coast of northern Asia it is up to 1,500 km (930 miles) wide, divided by islands and submarine ridges into several shallow seas that are among the world's richest fishing grounds. In summer they are fished by fleets from America, Iceland, northern Europe and the Soviet Union.

△ Even though protected by international agreement, whales are still hunted by many nations.

▽ Reindeer herding remains an important way of life in northern Scandinavia.

△ Drilling rigs on the waterlogged North Slope of Alaska are often built on artificial "islands" of sand.

△ Fishing boats and whale-catchers lie at anchor in the ice-littered harbor of Jakobshavn in west Greenland.

The continental shelf off Alaska has also been found to contain oilfields, and despite the harsh environment, several fields have already been developed. The oil is piped across the frozen tundra to ports on Alaska's southern coast.

The problem today is that man's activities are threatening to destroy the balance of nature in the Arctic. For thousands of years the Eskimo people lived by fishing and by hunting seals, whales and walruses. The Laplanders and the peoples of northern Asia also hunted, and tended huge herds of reindeer. Neither way of life damaged the environment because the people took no more than their daily needs.

Today commercial river fisheries and fish-canning factories have almost replaced the Eskimo way of life. Thousands of young seals are slaughtered every year, just for their silver fur. And if we continue to fish the Arctic seas faster than they can recover, one day there will be no more fish to be harvested.

25

The frozen continent

In any book of geographical records Antarctica rates several entries. It is the coldest place on earth, with a record low of −89.2°C. It is the windiest place on earth, with gales of more than 150 km/h (90 mph) sometimes lasting for a week or more. And it is the highest continent. Its great dome of ice reaches 2,700 m (8,860 ft) at its highest point, and the average height of the ice sheet is 2,000 m (6,560 ft) above sea level – even though the bedrock far beneath the ice is below sea level in many places. Finally, Antarctica has the world's southernmost volcano – the 3,795-m (12,450-ft) Mount Erebus on Ross Island.

The continent itself is poor in wildlife. There are no land animals, no trees, not even a blade of grass. Only on the subantarctic islands scattered across the southern oceans can tussock grass grow on the thin soils.

△ The rocky peaks of the Antarctic Peninsula and subantarctic islands like South Georgia provide some of the most beautiful scenery in Antarctica.

▽ Antarctica is surrounded by a wide pack-ice zone.

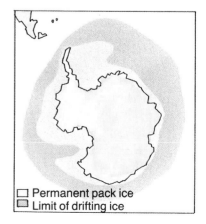

☐ Permanent pack ice
☐ Limit of drifting ice

These remote islands are the breeding grounds of the albatrosses, whose enormous wings carry them far and wide across the southern seas.

The only living creatures to be found on the continent are the birds and seals that crowd on to the rocky shores and offshore islands during the summer breeding season.

Most familiar of all are the penguins. Five of the sixteen species are truly Antarctic and of these the Adélie is the most common and most southerly. They come ashore in spring to breed in enormous colonies on low rocky islands, but then spend the rest of the year at sea.

The strangest oddity of all, however, is the magnificent emperor penguin, who chooses to breed at the end of summer. The female lays her egg and departs to sea, but the male spends the entire winter on the ice, cradling the single large egg between the tops of his leathery feet and the warm skin of his belly. The eggs hatch in spring – just when the ocean food supply is at its richest.

▽ Life in Antarctica is concentrated in the sea. Weddell seals, the most common species, can dive to 600 m (1,970 ft) and remain submerged for more than an hour. They stay in coastal waters throughout the year, feeding on fish and squid. The leopard seal is a swift, powerful hunter that lives in the pack-ice zone and feeds on fish, squid and penguins. The killer whale is the supreme hunter and the main enemy of seals.

A continent for science

At the beginning of this century Antarctica was like a magnet to explorers. Men like Shackleton, Scott and Amundsen risked everything to be first at the South Pole. Today the continent has been crossed and its mountains have been visited. Antarctica is now a continent for scientists.

For geologists there are still many questions to be answered about this remarkable land. Coal seams prove that part of it was once covered in swamp forests. Fossils show that at times it lay beneath warm shallow seas. And rock layers tell of many periods of violent volcanic activity and turbulent earth movements.

▽ While their supply ship ties up alongside the floating sea ice, men from a British research base prepare a safe route across the ice and up a natural slope or "ramp" to the top of the 40-m (130-ft) high ice cliff. Tractor-drawn sleds will carry the year's food and scientific supplies to the base, several miles away.

The animal life of Antarctica is full of interest and surprises for biologists – from the curious "ice fish", whose blood carries its own form of antifreeze, to the less welcome discovery that penguins in Antarctica had DDT in their body fat. The chemical had washed off farmland all over the world and had spread throughout the world's oceans.

Antarctica's glaciers and ice sheets provide a natural laboratory for glaciologists studying the movements of ice. Meteorologists go there to study the earth's weather systems. Climatologists investigate the mysteries of past Ice Ages, and other scientists explore the radiaton belts of the earth's upper atmosphere.

Today Antarctica is protected by an international treaty. Weapons tests and military uses are banned. The land may be used only for peaceful research in the earth sciences. That treaty is immensely important, for it protects one of the last great wilderness areas on earth.

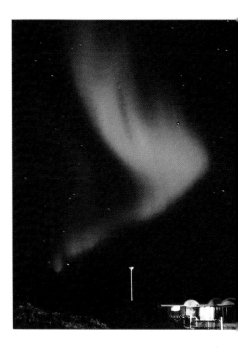

△ When electrically charged particles from the sun strike the thin gases of the upper atmosphere, the gases glow and create the "Southern Lights."

◁ A surveyor working on one of the Antarctic islands draws a "line of sight" showing the compass bearing of a hilltop measured from the survey point. Later these details will be used to draw a finished map of the area.

Arête A sharp knife-edge ridge formed in mountain scenery by the frost-shattering of the rocks and by the action of moving glacier ice.

Bergschrund The deep crevasse formed in the ice at the back of a cirque where the ice is separating from the rock of the back wall.

Boulder clay (also called till) The mass of clay, rock flour, sand and stones carried along by a glacier or ice sheet and dumped on the ground when the ice melts.

Cirque (also called a corrie) The deep, rounded, steep-walled hollow in a hillside or mountain formed by the head of a glacier.

Continental shelf The shallow platform of continental rock that extends out from the coast to a depth of about 200 m (650 ft). The edge of the shelf marks the true edge of the continent.

Crevasse A deep crack in the ice of a glacier or ice sheet, caused when the ice flows down a steep slope or around a sharp bend in its valley.

Drumlin A peculiar landscape feature consisting of groups of elongated low hills of boulder clay, smoothed and rounded by the ice sheet riding over them. The hills are shaped like half eggs and drumlin fields are sometimes called "basket of eggs" features.

Erosion The process of wearing away the rocks of the earth's crust. Wind erosion, river erosion and glacial erosion each produce their own characteristic landscape features.

Erratic A large piece of rock carried far from its place of origin by an ice sheet or glacier.

Esker A long winding ridge of sand and stones that marks where a river once flowed beneath a glacier.

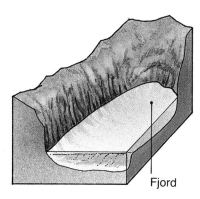
Fjord

Fjord A deep, steep-sided inlet in the coast, formed by the flooding of a valley widened and deepened by a glacier. Some of the most spectacular fjords are those of Norway and Greenland.

Glacier A slow-moving "river" of ice. The longest glacier is the Lambert Glacier in Antarctica. It is up to 65 km (40 miles) wide and more than 400 km (250 miles) long. One of its tributaries, the Fisher Glacier, starts high on the 3,355-m (11,000-ft) Mount Menzies. If this glacier is added, the total length of the ice-flow is 515 km (320 miles).

The longest mountain glacier is the Siachen Glacier in the Karakoram Range of the Himalayas. It is 75 km (47 miles) long.

Hanging valley A side valley that enters a main glaciated valley high up on the valley side rather than at the level of the valley floor. It marks the point where a small tributary glacier flowed into a main glacier.

Hibernation The process by which some animals build up their reserves of fat in the late summer and then spend the winter in a form of deep sleep.

Ice Age A period in the earth's past when large areas of land were covered by ice sheets. In the Carboniferous Period (345–280 million years ago) ice sheets covered parts of South America, most of southern Africa, all of India and the southern part of Australia – all of which were joined into one large land area at that time. The most recent Ice Age started about 1 million years ago and has probably not yet ended.

Iceberg A large block of floating ice that has broken off a glacier or ice shelf where it meets the sea. The largest iceberg on record was sighted in the South Pacific in 1956. It measured 335 km by 100 km (200 by 60 miles) and had an area larger than Belgium!

Ice cap A dome of ice filling in and covering up a large area of land. (*See also* ice sheet.)

Icefall A jumbled mass of ice blocks, separated by deep crevasses, formed where a glacier flows down a steep slope.

Ice sheet A very large ice cap, usually defined as one covering an area of more than 50,000 sq km (19,300 sq miles).

Ice shelf A thick sheet of floating ice attached to the coast. Ice shelves can be of enormous size: the leading edge of the Ross Ice Shelf in Antarctica forms an ice cliff 30 m (100 ft) high stretching for nearly 650 km (400 miles).

Marine Anything to do with the seas and oceans. For example, marine life, marine engineering, marine pollution.

Meltwater Any water that comes directly from the melting of ice.

Migration The regular, seasonal movements of animals, usually from a summer range to a winter range and back again. The most familiar migrants are birds, but migration is also common in fish, turtles and many mammals, from the arctic caribou to the zebra and wildebeest of East Africa.

Moraine The boulder clay and rock debris carried by a glacier and dropped when the ice melts. The three main types are **lateral** moraines, along the edge of a glacier; **medial** moraines, formed in mid-stream when two glaciers merge; and **end** moraines, also called terminal moraines, that are pushed along in front of the ice.

Névé (also called firn) The transition stage between hard-packed snow and clear ice.

Nunatak A sharp mountain peak poking up through an ice cap or ice sheet.

Pack ice Floating sea ice which forms in huge sheets in winter. They break up into floes and smaller pieces in summer, drifting on the wind and water currents until they melt or become frozen into the next year's ice.

Peninsula A long narrow piece of land jutting out into the sea. It can be a small, local coastal landmark or a very large geographical feature such as Italy or Baja California.

Permafrost Ground that is permanently frozen. In polar regions permafrost lies underneath the shallow surface layer that may soften during the summer.

Pingo A landscape feature of tundra regions. Water deep beneath the ground freezes, pushing the surface into a high mound.

Plateau A region of high land, usually flat-topped or nearly so and surrounded by steep slopes falling to the lowlands below.

Ribbon lake A long, very narrow lake occupying a glacial valley or trough.

Rock flour The very fine powdered rock formed by the grinding action of a moving glacier.

Scree The mass of loose rocks and boulders that accumulates at the bottom of a cliff or steep slope when there is no river or sea to carry the debris away. Scree slopes, or talus slopes, are very unstable: any slight movement can set the whole mass sliding downhill.

Snout The name given to the end of a glacier.

Temperate The word means "moderate" and is used for the middle latitude zone between the Arctic regions and the hot, moist tropics. Temperate regions have seasonal weather variations with warm dry summers and cool wet winters.

Tundra The harsh landscape lying between the edge of the polar ice and the northern limit of the coniferous forest belt.

Index